D1414848

How to Be the Perfect Grandma

BRYNA NELSON PASTON

Copyright © 2002, 2010, 2018 by Bryna Nelson Paston
Cover and internal design © 2018 by Sourcebooks, Inc.
Cover design by Krista Joy Johnson
Cover image © nelik/GettyImages
Internal images © stasia_ch/Shutterstock; Angeliki Vel/Shutterstock

Sourcebooks and the colophon are registered trademarks of Sourcebooks, Inc.

All rights reserved. No part of this book may be reproduced in any form or by any electronic or mechanical means including information storage and retrieval systems—except in the case of brief quotations embodied in critical articles or reviews—without permission in writing from its publisher, Sourcebooks, Inc.

All brand names and product names used in this book are trademarks, registered trademarks, or trade names of their respective holders. Sourcebooks, Inc., is not associated with any product or vendor in this book.

Published by Sourcebooks, Inc.
P.O. Box 4410, Naperville, Illinois 60567-4410
(630) 961-3900
Fax: (630) 961-2168
sourcebooks.com

Library of Congress Cataloging-in-Publication Data is on file with the publisher.

Printed and bound in the United States of America.
VP 10 9 8 7 6 5 4 3 2 1

Dedicated to all those I love who made me
what I am today—a very happy grandma:

Alexis, Amanda, Jake, Kelsey, Matt, and Rachel; their terrific
parents, Michael and Carrie, Dina and Brent;

and, of course, Grandpa Alan.

⤳ CONTENTS ⤶

❧ STANDING BY ❧

When our first grandchild was about to enter our world, my son Michael called and told us they were off to the hospital and we should "stand by."

I don't do "stand by" very well so I jumped in my car and zoomed to the hospital (just a tad over the speed limit) and began searching for the father- and mother-to-be. Michael came out of the delivery room to announce that Rachel was forty-five minutes old and beautiful. I hugged him like never before and suddenly, in my mind, he was just born forty-five minutes ago; then he was a toddler, a first grader, a senior in high school, a college grad, and a man.

A funny thing happened to my first-born son when he had his first (and only) daughter. Michael became the self-appointed father of the year. He knew everything there was to know about fathering. As for me, the instant grandma, I knew nothing. Never mind that I raised him. I no longer knew anything about raising anybody, and he declared me brain-dead. Michael was in charge of Rachel. He had rules for taking care of her. And all of them applied to me.

Therefore, I started taking notes. Along the way I added my friends' stories about grandparenting. Their first-time grandma stories were as funny as mine. Thankfully, I learned I wasn't the only grandma declared brain-dead by my kid. There were a lot of us running around creating chaos. It was an epidemic of know-nothing grandmas who needed to learn a whole lot about taking care of babies. It tickled my fancy and my funny bone.

There was only one way to get even. I took pen to paper—or, as in this new millennium, fingertips to keyboard—and I wrote this book. Luckily, my son Michael has a sense of humor.

The "rules and regulations" slowly disappeared when Michael's son Jake was born, and by the time their third child, Matt, was here, they were such laid-back parents, they would give me the kids on a moment's notice. As they pulled out of the driveway after dropping my grandkids off one afternoon, they yelled, "Have fun, don't bring them back until next week, and do anything you want."

Meanwhile, our daughter Dina married and produced three daughters bing, bang, boom. Kelsey and Amanda are eighteen months apart and Alexis is two years younger. I think she trusted me more with her kids than Michael did with his. But still, I gathered more and more stories to be told.

I have a wonderful time as a grandmother. By the grace of God, our grandkids live close by and I never stop thinking how lucky I am to have them. I have been a spectator at most of their games and shows, and I have been a participant in so much more, which you will learn as you read my book.

I have watched them grow into fascinating teenagers, each with his or her distinct personality. I will tell you this much—they can laugh at themselves as much as at each other—and they certainly can laugh with me. I am not as involved in their lives as I used to be, and a part of me wishes we could go back. But life just happens and they grow up as you grow old.

I try to stay connected any which way I can, and it's hard

sometimes. I know they still love me, but their lives have taken on a force of nature that doesn't include Grandma. We'll be closer again, I'm sure of it. Basically, I am standing by.

❧ GRANDMOTHERING HAS ITS PERKS ❧

Speaking of laughs—and we are—when my son Michael and daughter-in-law Carrie came back after a five-day vacation, they were truly grateful for my baby-sitting. They brought me a jar of marmalade—in its original jar, unwrapped, a pleasant shade of orange. They knew I hadn't had it easy. Rachel was sick in bed the whole time, and Jake got into trouble with the police. She was three and he was eighteen months old. (See Rule 21 for the rest of the story!)

It wasn't exactly a stress-free period for Grandma. But their kids were fed, sheltered, clothed appropriately, pampered, and relatively safe.

I have many grandma friends who baby-sit like me. Their kids come back with beautiful thank-you gifts: Faith got an Italian leather pocketbook. Carole got a beautiful handcrafted pin. I got marmalade. Faith and Carole, not to mention Suzie, Marcia, Irene, and Marilyn, are insane with jealousy. They may never get over it. *I got marmalade!*

I still have it—seven years later—untouched, uneaten, unopened, prominently displayed in my breakfront alongside the Baccarat crystal. It is one of my most cherished possessions. It's easy to give Grandma an Italian pocketbook of buttery soft leather or a unique piece of fine gold jewelry. But when you get marmalade, you feel truly appreciated.

I only hoped that when they went away and we babysat the following year, and the next, and the next, and the next, they would bring back something just as special to express their gratitude. I've been praying for guava jelly. Maybe this year.

The Rules

Rule 1

There are rules. Follow them or go directly to Grandma jail.

When she was five, my darling, precious, brilliant, beautiful granddaughter Rachel said, "You can't be a grandma unless you are a ma first." I only wish it were the reverse. I should have been a grandma right after college and before my kids got in the way.

Becoming a grandmother is not one of life's free choices. You can pick your pet, your alma mater, and your spouse. You can decide when to have kids and how many, if you're careful. In the professional world, you can be a doctor, lawyer, mountain climber, or plumber.

But when and where you become a grandma is solely your kids' decision. Now that I have six grandchildren, ages three through ten, I say to anyone who will listen, "My kids finally got something right."

Becoming a grandma is like getting a subpoena. You don't expect it; you don't know how to respond; you know you must be mature. You know you must accept it or the sheriff won't go away.

Truth be told, being a grandma is as close as we ever get to perfection. The ultimate warm sticky bun with plump raisins and nuts. Clouds nine, ten, and eleven.

There is only one little problem—the generation in the middle. Dealing with your kid and your kid's mate while you become the most relevant person in your grandchild's life is tricky at best, and downright impossible at worst.

If they would just leave us alone—us and the little kids—we would be just fine. No one would break out in hives, no one would get lost, no one would die. But *there are rules*, and you, as the grandparent, must follow those rules or go directly to jail.

Make your move fast and decisively.

My friend Adele has a daughter-in-law who is a doctor, and after being home with her son his first six months, she wanted to go back to work. So daughter-in-law called mother-in-law and invited her to come to her office and take care of little Jeffrey while she worked at her busy medical practice. "What? Sit all day in your office? Are you crazy?" Adele refused—nicely.

So the mommy/doctor decided to hire a nanny, but since she still needed Adele two mornings a week before the nanny could get there, she asked her to baby-sit from 7:00 to 9:00 a.m. Adele said okay—happily. But first, Adele had to audition. She was instructed to arrive at their house by 6:00 a.m. while the mommy and daddy were still home to supervise. Adele had to take charge of the baby under the watchful eyes of his parents, just so they could be sure she knew what she was doing. The first morning the audition never even got off the ground because the baby slept through the whole experience, and Mommy and Daddy watched Adele watch them.

The next audition took place a week later—same time, same place, same result. Baby Jeffrey snoozed. Always one to find the silver lining, Adele decided it wasn't so crazy— after all, the best part of the day was ahead of her. She was up and dressed and out before the birds. I never heard if Adele made the cut, or if she ever went back, or if she just lay down next to her grandson and took a well-deserved nap.

Or if she said, like any sensible woman in her middle years would, "I was a mother before I became a grandmother, and I've noticed that you and your siblings have grown up to get married and hold down jobs. You aren't forever lost in the woods, you usually can tell right from wrong, and the hives cleared up years ago. I think I know what I'm doing, and to tell the truth, you don't."

Of course, we never say that. Frankly, I am not the least interested in what my kids (now fortysomethings) have to say about parenting. I care only about their offspring. We have a window of opportunity as grandparents—usually the first five years, maybe more if you're lucky. My Rachel still likes me and she's ten, but by the time you read this, she'll be playing softball every day, chatting up Prince William on the Internet, or giggling with her girlfriends, and she won't have much time for Grandma.

So you have to make your move fast and decisively. Your kids and/or their spouses will intrude, interrupt, and interfere. They will be a pain in the you-know-what. But persevere, circumvent them, do exactly what you want, and lie (with dignity) when needed. The rewards are stupendous. You and your grandchildren will be glued together forever. My friend Irene (grandmother of four, one in college) tells me I am busy making "criers" for my funeral—she's right. These six very grand kids are really going to miss me when I'm gone.

As for your kids, they'll manage to survive your "intrusion" as a grandmother because if they have a brain in their collective head, they'll realize your presence gives them their freedom. They should kiss the ground you walk on.

Rule 3

Be calm. Pick your battles. Trust me, you'll have plenty.

When Rachel was a baby, she was not allowed to stay overnight at our house because we have a cat. The cat, who is afraid of his own shadow, might jump in the crib and smother her, not to mention all the cat hair she would ingest while she slept. So they brought her for daytime visits only and she napped in someone's arms.

I said, "No problem." I kept my cool and let them have their way. Never mind that I had a crib, mattress, bumper pad, and mobile (black and white, of course) placed in a quiet room with good ventilation and a night-light. Rachel was six months old before she was allowed to set foot in that crib.

I considered killing the cat, but I really like him.

Rachel's younger brother Jake was born to the very same

parents, and at the ripe old age of one month, he was in that very same crib, comfy as a kitty.

My friend Faith used to say, "I wish my kids would hurry up and have a second child so I can get the first." Faith is one smart cookie—she knows that they will ease up considerably with the second. So if your kids are lunatics about the first, wait!

Be calm. Pick your battles. Trust me, you'll have plenty.

Rule 4

Promise anything, but get the kid.

One night in a severe rainstorm, my son Michael packed up eight-month-old Rachel and buckled her into my Jeep so I could take her home for a sleepover. "It's really raining hard, Mom," said Michael.

"I know, Sweetheart," I answered.

"Well, drive carefully. [Afterthought] Precious cargo, you know," he said with a worried expression.

"Oh, so glad you reminded me," I said with the utmost sincerity. Of course I drove at the breakneck speed of fifteen miles an hour and stopped for every yellow light.

If you want the kid, promise to protect her, defend her, and sacrifice your life for her (which you would do a hundred times over). Promise anything, but get the kid.

Rule 5

Shut up and leave.

As I was pulling out of the driveway to take Rachel for our sleepover, Michael waved for my attention.

"Oh, Mom." One last thought from the daddy. "Don't do Rachel's laundry."

"How come?" I asked.

"Because you don't do it right," he replied.

I could have sat with the motor running while we discussed my laundry skills, and I could have pointed out that I had washed, dried, fluffed, and folded his underwear for eighteen years and his clothes were in pristine condition at all times. And we could have debated the merits of separating whites and colors or exactly what kind of detergent is best.

Or I could have done exactly what I did: shut my mouth and just left.

Rule 6

Don't even answer the phone when you've got the baby. Let Grandpa talk to them. They never mess with him.

Daddy called seven times that night. "Is everything okay?" he asked.

"Just fine," I said cheerfully.

"Now don't say everything is fine if it isn't."

"Honestly, Michael, everything is fine."

"Is she sleeping? Was she fussy? Did she finish her bottle? Don't give her an extra."

"Yes. No. Yes. Okay," I answered.

"She might get up in the night," he continued.

"So I'll get up with her," I said.

"Well, that would be good," he said. "But don't keep her up. It's the middle of the night, you know."

"Yes, dear," I said and hung up.

Rule 7

Never, ever, ever let anything bad happen to the kid on your watch. But if it does, lie.

When Jake, now seven, was about ten months old, I was baby-sitting him and his older sister Rachel. We had been out and about, and when we got home, I carried Jake inside, still buckled into his car seat, and put him on top of the kitchen counter (his parents, I might point out, did this all the time without incident). I gave him a bottle and turned for a nanosecond toward Rachel to help her untie her shoe. Jake careened off the counter. Splat! Face-down on the floor with the car seat still fastened to his back.

He started screaming, which was the only good sign. At least he was conscious.

"Grandma, Jake fell," Rachel enlightened me.

"I know, Rache." My heart raced and sweat popped out of every pore. I'm sure I was ashen with fear; my mouth was so dry I could hardly swallow. My mind galloped—should I call somebody? Who? No neighbors around. It was 11 a.m. on a Tuesday. Should I scoop him up and go directly to a hospital? What hospital? I didn't even know where one was. The mall I knew, but the hospital?

Oh, did I forget to mention that my daughter-in-law is an emergency physician? I didn't even know where her hospital was, and besides, she was out on the golf course where she belonged, while I was the one having the emergency. I thought about calling my husband, the sane one. He'd know what to do. But he was forty-five minutes away dealing with customers, and even if he left somebody on hold he wouldn't get here in time.

No. I just picked Jake up, unbuckled him, and tried to inspect the damage. He was screaming. I held him and patted him and talked to him, and to God. I walked and talked and prayed like never before.

"Grandma, Jake fell off the counter," repeated wide-eyed Rachel.

"He'll be fine. Just fine," I said over and over. I'll never get away with this one, my brain said over and over.

He had a serious red mark on his forehead, but no broken nose or other marks on that beautiful face. All right, it's only eleven o'clock. They'll play eighteen holes for sure. They won't be home before six. God and I can work this out by then.

I iced him. I soothed him. I sang to him. All the while, Rachel hovered. "He's fine, Rache. Just fine," I tried to reassure one of us.

Eventually, the hysterical crying subsided. The red lump was the size of a peach, but he acted normally. When I put him down for a nap (the first time I let go of him all day), I sat on the floor beside his crib and watched him sleep.

The minute my son and daughter-in-law arrived, I fessed right up, knowing that Rachel, the little snitch, was going to turn me in.

"Ummmm, Jake had a little accident, but he's fine," I said, picking up the child, Exhibit A. "The lump is almost gone. He'll be fine."

"Mom, Jake fell off the counter," Rachel piped up helpfully. "In his car seat," she added.

"What?" shouted the daddy. "He *fell*? What? Why weren't you watching him, Mom?" All my stammering wasn't going to make a bit of difference. *"He fell off the counter?"* Michael said even louder this time, waving his arms.

I knew exactly what he was thinking. He was thinking about the time twenty-five years ago when he and his younger sister Dina and I were in a mall, and Dina suddenly disappeared. Michael yelled at me then too. He was seven and very responsible; she was four and curious. We ran in and out of stores for twenty minutes until an elderly man sitting on a bench under a fake palm tree asked us if we were looking for a little girl, and then kindly pointed out which store she was in. We found her, perfectly fine and happy. She didn't know she was lost. God watches over incompetent mothers, little kids, and drunks—you can add grandmothers to that list too, please.

Let me reassure you that God is on your side. And as I tried to explain to my son, parents lose kids all the time. It's one of life's little adventures.

Back to present, he was still ranting when my daughter-in-law chimed in. "Jake's okay, Mike. I think I'll go upstairs and take a shower. Thanks for watching them," she said to me calmly as she headed up the stairs.

"Any time," I answered weakly, knowing full well I was about to be banished from the kingdom forever.

An enraged Michael continued bellowing, "Mom, I don't understand it. How could you leave him alone in the car seat on the counter?"

"He *wasn't* alone," I said. "I just looked away for a second, that's all. I'm sorry. I hate myself. I don't want anything bad to happen to your children. It won't happen again. I promise. I swear. No, I don't swear. I'm not supposed to swear in front of the children. I will live with this forever, and that is punishment enough."

By the look on his face, I could tell that putting me on the rack without food or water for ninety years wouldn't be punishment enough.

A couple of days later, when life was calmer, I prepared a gourmet feast for them. I decided to try to turn this incident around.

"You know," I began as I heaped mounds of my famous chicken salad with grapes on their plates, "when I am alone here with the kids, and I can't reach you on the fifteenth hole, and if there is a *real* emergency—as opposed to this one, which was nothing—I don't even have the neighbors' numbers."

"Call 911," my daughter-in-law, Carrie, said calmly.

"Yes, I know about 911," I said. "But what if it's really serious and I need to just get the kid, or I mean somebody here like a visitor who is having a heart attack, to the hospital as quickly as possible. I don't know where it is."

"Follow the H," my daughter-in-law said calmly.

Of course, first I'd have to find the signs on the road with the "H" leading to the nearest hospital.

My son continued eating in silence. Icicles were dripping from his brow. He wouldn't even look at me.

The moral of this story is never, ever, ever let anything bad happen to the kids on your watch. But as we all know, bad things happen to good grandmothers. So, if it's just you and the child, lie. If another child sees it all, try to fix the blame on anything or anybody you can come up with. It's her word against yours, and you are the adult here...I think. Example: "There was a small fire in the trash can and I had to put it out, and in that instant, Jake fell off the counter." Or, "He is sooooooo strong, that baby—he kicked me in the belly and propelled himself right off the counter."

Rule 8

Do whatever is necessary for the good of your grandchild.

Rachel got the chickenpox from her mommy who got them from God knows who or what in the emergency room where she works (and I still don't know how to get there!). All right, of all the possible horrendous diseases or bullets she could catch in the "Knife and Gun Club," as the insiders call it, chickenpox is the very least of it.

Mommy was sick, but she toughed it out. Rachel, at a year and a half, was sicker than sick, so they called in the National Guard—Grandma!

It was a dark and stormy night. Mom was working. Dad was sleeping. Grandma and Rachel were walking the floors. She was burning up with fever so I couldn't and wouldn't put her down. We rocked and walked; I sang and talked into the wee hours. Daddy was there among us, sleeping loudly, snoring like a steam engine. I was reminded of when Michael was a little boy. He was kind of quiet during the day, but when he slept, he filibustered. Hardly any of it was coherent, so I never did learn his deepest, darkest secrets.

Now, here we are—fast-forward to the next generation. My son the daddy and his daughter, my first grandchild. I'm rocking and walking and he's sleeping and sleeping. "Daddy snoring loud," said Rachel as she clung to my neck.

"What's wrong with this picture?" I asked no one in particular.

The next day, Daddy went to work; Mommy came home after her shift and went to sleep. Rachel and I had a picnic in the bed, watched cartoons, and slept off and on. The next day everyone was better, except Grandma, who finally went home to drop dead until Tuesday.

No matter what is needed from Grandma, if it's for the good and welfare of your grandchild, *do it!* The beauty of being a grandmother is you can go home and pass out later.

Rule 9

Listen politely to instructions, then do what you want. Just like your kids did to you.

When Rachel was about a year old, we asked to take her to the beach, just an hour away. When we picked her up, her daddy said, "I'm not giving you her stroller because it's too windy for her on the boardwalk."

"Okay," we said, smiling cheerfully.

When we arrived in Atlantic City we immediately bought a stroller and took her on the boardwalk. She loved every minute, and the wind didn't blow her out to sea. We never told, and she couldn't talk yet.

Rule 10

Her mother is blood.
His is company.

My friend Suzie had a granddaughter out of town, her first. Suzie sees her often because she takes a day off, schleps three hours in the car, stays overnight, and gets up early enough to get back to her desk by 9 a.m.

"I called and asked if I could come next week to see the baby and they said no," Suzie told me one day. Then Suzie said, "No????"

"No," said her firstborn son, the attorney, married to an emergency physician. (I know it's bizarre, but we're having an epidemic. The son of one of my dearest friends is in the same profession as mine and married to yet another bionic woman who runs an ER! Suzie and I relate on many levels.)

"No????" Suzie asked, her voice rising.

"No," he replied again.

Well, they kept up this clever banter until my friend Suzie changed her "No???" to "Why not?"

Her son said, "We've had too much company lately."

"I am not company," Suzie stated emphatically. "I am the grandmother."

The answer? "Sorry, Mom."

Always remember: If you are the mother-in-law of the mother of your grandchild, you are company, now and forever more. Repeat one hundred times: I AM COMPANY. *Her* mother is blood. His is company.

Since that time, Suzie's son and daughter-in-law have had two more daughters. But here's the good news: Suzie's daughter got married and had a baby. There is a difference, folks. If you are the mother of the mother, you've pretty much got carte blanche, but if you are the mother of the daddy, you tiptoe through the tulips. Luckily, I have a daughter with three little girls, and she trusts me implicitly with her kids—I think. In the beginning, when there was only Kelsey (now six), my daughter Dina gave me one rule: no pacifier after 9 p.m. I'll let you know when I figure that one out. I suppose after a certain time, pacifiers melt.

Rule 11

Ignore the pacifier.

On the subject of pacifiers: they do not use it for the first child, occasionally for the second, and the third is allowed to suck up a storm. Pacifier use is directly linked to the level of stress in the house and the condition of the mother's nerve endings.

Yes, I know it's a killer, but ignore the pacifier. It will go away. I can't think of one child in a cap and gown sucking on a pacifier. If you absolutely must tell someone that you raised your children without a pacifier and it really is the most disgusting thing on earth, and why do these kids give their kids one since we wouldn't have dreamed of it, call a friend.

Rule 12

They do not sterilize bottles
or boil nipples anymore.

It's twenty seconds in the microwave if they heat the bottle at all. As my daughter Dina pointed out, nobody grows up and eats cookies and warm milk before bed. (Well, if you're eighty-seven and your stomach is on the fritz, maybe!)

Rule 13

Babies sleep propped on their sides or backs.

Don't even think about putting "Precious" on his tummy. This topic concerns life and death, so you comply without a whimper. The only hitch is that it takes a little practice to get that receiving blanket rolled up into the perfect shape, then you push the baby into position, trying to keep all four limbs free. When you step back to admire your handiwork, you'll swear that Baby will be so uncomfortable that he won't sleep a wink. He will, and you should lie down too. You may sleep any old way you want, even on your stomach. The key here is to keep breathing.

Baby powder is passé.

Done! Finished! Gone! They determined out there in Healthy Babyland that baby powder gets into the lungs and causes serious problems. The baby's bottom gets a good application of air once in a while, and that's it. I try to imagine what my children's lungs must look like with layers upon layers of baby powder dust just sitting there, and believe me, it's an ugly sight.

Now, if you think that when you get the baby alone, you'll just sprinkle a little Johnson & Johnson's on her bottom for old time's sake and because it smells really good, think again. That baby will ingest the powder and every organ in her body will be clogged forever. You won't be able to hide this one—baby powder lingers in their drool.

Rule 15

The playpen is out; the entire house is in.

Speaking of baby accessories, tools, and equipment that are obsolete, consider the playpen. I imagine that they sell one every two or three years nationwide. Don't go out and buy one. It's never used. Today's enlightened parents prefer to give their offspring the run (or crawl) of the house, so they don't stifle their "creativity."

The playpen is out, walkers are dangerous, bottles no longer need to be warmed, nipples don't need to be sterilized, we already discussed baby powder, and you don't need to buy a car seat. Just switch cars with the parents so when you get the baby you also get the SUV all belted and buckled.

Rule 16

You are no longer the reigning monarch.

You don't even have a monarchy anymore. You used to be in charge. You made sensible rules for your kids. Look both ways, don't talk with your mouth full, don't kill each other, wash your hands after using the potty, be helpful to others, think before you speak.

Well, it worked. You raised two or three (maybe more, God help you) who turned out okay. Full-blown adults—sometimes! Now, *they* are in charge, and *they* are making the rules for their kids.

You have become the dowager queen, if you're lucky, and you don't make rules. It's not in your job description. You don't even have an opinion, except when discussing discipline with your fellow grandmas. Then, you have forty-seven opinions (or more, if they'll listen).

My dear friend Carole says her grandchildren are under-disciplined. "They're hanging from the chandeliers," she says. "My daughter-in-law is very laid-back."

I, on the other hand, have General Georgette Patton for a daughter-in-law, and I reply with a hint of smugness, "Oh, my grandchildren on my son's side really toe the line."

Sometimes you get caught in the wave of discipline and all you want to do is swim to a safer shore. My grandson Jake, during that Terrible Two Time, decided one night to write all over the kitchen floor with a permanent marker. I was a hostile witness for the prosecution. Even so, Jake was punished. He had to take a time-out, he was banished to the sofa until further notice, and he lost dessert privileges for the rest of his natural life. From his isolated outpost, he peeked over the top of the sofa with those big blues brimming over with tears. In between heart-wrenching sobs, he pleaded with me to save him. I'll never forget that plaintive "GRAAAANMOM!"

But of course, communication was out of the question. I had to be strong. I silently turned and left the room. I left the house, the township, the county, and the state before I cried in the car all the way home.

Rule 17

MYOB

Unless, of course, they are with you in your house and you are back in charge. My grandchildren have a playroom in my house, and they can rock and roll all day and all night there. They eat in that room. They sleep with us on the sleeper sofa. We have picnics in the bed, and we stay up till all hours watching videos or telling funny stories. They feed our cat; they vie over which child can empty the poopy box. Honest.

"There is one big rule in my house," I said early on. "No whining at Grandma's." If you happen to run into Rachel, Jake, Matt, Kelsey, Amanda, or Alexis one day, they will tell you, emphatically I hope, *"No whining at Grandma's."*

Rule 18

Grandma's house should always be stocked with the good stuff.

When and if the kidlets are allowed to come to your house, be prepared. You don't want them to catch you with fewer toys than the nearest retail outlet. In my case, I update for the oldest and keep everything on hand—within easy reach—for every age.

I have a huge toy box for the older kids and a cute toy chest for the younger ones. I have a closet stocked with books, games, and puzzles that I pick up at flea markets, garage sales, and discount stores. I maintain a box of dress-up clothes and shoes (outcasts from my own closet). I've stocked a drawer with old costume jewelry that I keep within everyone's reach. Of course, they only want to wear the real jewelry and they know which drawer it's in—I do let them, but I supervise. I have tub toys and a canister I keep full of Tootsie Pops or other like snacks.

I have a used crib, borrowed from my friend Irene, a high chair, a booster, and a gate for the steps. I have bottles (no longer needed) and sippy cups (they have a long life because they can be carried upside down throughout the house without fear of spillage). I keep apple juice, soda, and Pop-Tarts on hand in case of surprise visits.

I have personalized toothbrushes—one for each child and one for me and Grandpa that say "Grandma" and "Grandpa." If your grandchild has an unusual moniker like Magnolia Marie, first tell your kids that they saddled their kid with a name that will drive her crazy her whole life—like my dear departed parents did to me—then get creative. Make a name tag for a plain toothbrush. You would be surprised at how much it means to them to come over to Grandma's and look in the closet to find their own monogrammed toothbrush. And don't wait until they have teeth. The youngest of my brood, Alexis, was brushing right along with her sisters and cousins when she only had gums.

I have two step stools so they can reach the sink, and they know where I keep them. One of them, a battered, beaten, and weathered stool I can't bear to part with, was originally a baby gift for Michael (now thirty-six years old, and I'm happy to say, completely toilet trained and able to reach the sink).

Rule 19

You don't get a treat when your grandchild attempts a potty break. You only get wet.

Okay, now we'll move on to that terribly touchy subject of toilet training.

Your adult children will never, ever, ever toilet train their kids at the same age you toilet trained them. Don't even go there. You will never, ever, ever win this one. Just go with the program, even if they don't have one.

That is not to say that you won't find yourself trapped in the middle of your grandchildren's toilet training experience. You absolutely will. Put money on it.

I was holding Jake on my lap one day, admiring his "big boy" underpants, when he mentioned *the potty*. I raced him to the bathroom, nearly breaking my neck in the process, positioned him, and holding him so he wouldn't fall in, whispered words of encouragement and sang potty songs.

(I make this stuff up. There really isn't any catchy potty song out there that I would recommend.)

He announced with a triumphant grin that he was "allllllllll done" after ten seconds, so I picked him up, told him he was an exceptionally wonderful little person because he told me he had to go, and carried him back to the kitchen.

Suddenly I felt a warm, wet sensation all down the front of me, so we raced back to the bathroom. Too late, of course. I was soaked, the floor was soaked, and the big boy pants were soaked. The toilet remained unpolluted. There was nothing to do but comfort Jake, wash and dry him, and put another pair of big boy pants on him. After all, he had the concept.

Now, the parents and big sister arrive home. "I made peepee in the potty," he screamed with delight. Mom, Dad, and Rachel went nuts. Jake got a piece of gum as a reward. Don't ask me why, but Rachel got a piece of gum too. So I enthusiastically entered into the festivities after I mopped up the floor and changed my clothes. I didn't get a piece of gum.

Rule 20

Do not baby-sit unless you want to.

Let's revisit the baby-sitting issue for a moment. To sit or not to sit is a common problem shared by all grandparents. Stop torturing yourself and realize this: baby-sitting is a volunteer project. Period.

Do not baby-sit at your house or theirs if you don't want to. For your own sake, and because you don't want to hear every day and night from your friends how your kids take advantage of you, only baby-sit when it suits you or in dire emergencies. Of course, this approach is fraught with danger. In the event you suffer a long illness, you will need the baby-sitting services of your kids. They might say in your time of need, "We don't want to take care of you today, Mom. Empty your own bedpan."

Rule 21

Only let the child play with the cell phone.

We baby-sat once for Rachel and Jake when their parents took a golfing vacation to Florida. Rachel was three and Jake was about a year old. Rachel had a bad cold so she was tucked into my bed out of harm's way. Jake was sitting on the floor punching the buttons on the phone (the real one). I was there too, folding laundry.

All was peaceful and serene until I heard a shout from downstairs. I ran to look and found a very agitated young policeman in my living room.

"Did someone here call 911?" he demanded. "Ma'am, are you the only person in this house?"

Was he totally nuts? I stammered and stuttered, "No sir, I didn't call 911, sir. How did you get in my living room?"

"You have a note on the door to come in, it's open, and don't ring the bell, so I didn't," he said.

Oh, oh, right on, Mr. Swat Team. I did leave such a note because I didn't want doorbells ringing at nap time. I remained puzzled and silent.

"So who called 911?" he demanded more vehemently. "We tried to call back, but the line was busy."

Uh-oh, Jake was playing with the telephone. He couldn't possibly have randomly punched 911, could he? No, no this isn't happening. Do you go to jail for this?

"My grandson was doodling with the telephone, Officer, sir." I attempted an explanation. I could see by his expression he either didn't believe me altogether or he feared the ax murderer was lurking somewhere in the house, and I was covering my bases to convince him to leave, as per the intruder's instructions—at gunpoint.

"Do you realize the probability of a fine for a false alarm?" he said. Okay, maybe he did believe me.

"And do you realize the probability of my grandson randomly dialing 911?" I wasn't going to let him intimidate me!

"Mrs. Paston (he knew my real name!), is there anyone else in this house?" he asked.

"Just my two grandchildren, sir." I was contrite.

"Well, you should train your grandchildren not to play with the telephone, ma'am," he said. "It's not a toy, you know."

I should have already mentioned that my freewheeling attitude toward grandparenting sometimes gets me in trouble with the law. The kids can do anything at Grandma's—they can play with the phone, put the cat in the dryer, create confusion, drink, smoke, and tell dirty jokes.

"I know that, Officer," I said. "My grandson is only a year old. He's not even potty trained, much less phone trained."

He didn't believe me. I should have produced Jake right then and there, but I didn't think of it. And besides, he was on the phone randomly making obscene calls.

The policeman reprimanded me further, telling me how they had to follow up on every 911 call because you never know when someone is in real trouble, being held hostage, and what have you. And I should take his visit very seriously.

"I won't give you a fine this time." (Hallelujah!) "But be sure to take the phone away from that kid."

So remember: only let the child play with the cell phone. Then the cops won't be able to find you.

When I told the story to Michael and Carrie, they laughed till they cried. Finally, Michael said, "Jake must have been calling for help, Mom. What did you do to him?"

One of Michael's most endearing qualities is his sense of humor, which was evidenced by the gift I received from him and his wife when they returned from their vacation.

Rule 22

We all know that you are the better grandma, but try not to flaunt it when the competition is around.

By the time my daughter Dina had her first child, a daughter named Kelsey, I had Rachel and Jake under complete control. I was an experienced grandmother. But the old pro wasn't quite ready for the emotional upheaval of her daughter having a daughter.

First, she didn't exactly drop this baby on a lily pad. It took thirty-six hours of mild to brutal labor to get her into this world, and it would have been a lot easier on me if I had given birth instead of Dina. Once she arrived, Kelsey was fine. Mom had a sore bottom and I was in charge. I stayed with them (my son-in-law Brent and I had mucho bonding time—lucky guy!) in Connecticut in their teensy-weensy apartment, three flights up, for three weeks.

I shopped, ran errands, rocked the baby, washed the

clothes, told Dina she should reconsider and have more children later (stay tuned—she actually took my advice that time!), and got take-out every night for dinner.

We laughed, we cried, we talked forever, and I dispensed all the advice on mothering I could muster. After a while, my Visa card had a significant dent in it, and it was time for Dina and Brent to captain their own ship. I kissed them good-bye and drove three hours home down I-95, crying my heart out. I returned a month later and by then, Dina was the old pro.

When you have a grandchild and you are the mother of the baby's father, you are in a different position from when the baby's mother is your very own flesh and blood. You must and should behave differently. I am lucky enough to be both. However, if you only have sons—like my friend Marilyn—pray for granddaughters. It's your only hope.

Daughters-in-law come prepackaged, all wrapped up with their own mothers. Even though we know you are the better grandma, try not to show it when her mother is around. And this is important: check periodically with your grandchildren to make sure you are winning the grandma race. If by chance they say they like the other one better, buy them something they've been yearning for. And try harder.

Rule 23

Guilt-trip your daughter into having kids if you have to.

My friend Marilyn now has two grandchildren—a boy and a girl. But for years, she had none. At every opportunity I showed her thousands of pictures of mine, and she tried really hard to humor me. Just when she was about to give up, she decided she and her husband Paul would give themselves a grandparents' day—go to the zoo, play the kids' board game Crackers in the Bed, and stage a tea party. They just wanted to pretend. But as fate would have it, their good deeds and playful attitude paid off. At this writing, they have two, but there'll be more in store. As for me, I'm out of the baby business, I fear. We've signed off at six.

If you have a daughter without kids, tell her you have great expectations and your grandmother clock is ticking louder than her biological clock. Lay on a giant guilt trip about all you did for her. And couldn't she do this one little, tiny favor for you?

If it's your daughter-in-law who is stalling, tell your son there is an undisclosed sum of money in a Swiss bank account in his name, to be accessed only when they produce a child. And there is a deadline, of course. You are not waiting forever. Well, actually you are. The only other option if your own kids choose to remain childless is to divorce your husband and marry another man, one with grandchildren.

Rule 24

Always remember that you're in competition with the other grandmother.

My daughter-in-law's parents live five hours away. They do visit often, but they are cheated out of the spontaneity that we enjoy. And it doesn't matter where my daughter's in-laws live. They'll never be as good as us. I already told you that the daughter's mother lives a charmed life.

We try not to visit our son's children when his in-laws are on the scene. They deserve their own uninterrupted time when they come for the weekend. I came to this conclusion when we walked in after Carrie's parents had arrived the day before. The kids dropped them like hot potatoes and ran to us. Sonia, their *other* grandma, said plaintively, "I've been playing Barbies with Rachel for five hours and all you had to do was walk in the door."

If this happens, launch into a big speech about how it's

all about quality time, not quantity time. You and the other grandma both know you don't mean a word of it, but making nice is important.

"This is not a competition, Sonia," I told her. But of course it is, and I'm winning.

"You're the best grandma in the whole world," Sonia tells me. She is a much more gracious person than I am. "So are you, Sonia," I tell her back.

Rule 25

It doesn't matter what you do or where you live. It only matters that your title is "grandma."

Yes, I turn handsprings for my grandchildren. We take them to museums, plays, movies, zoos, and anything that's fun for kids. We have sleepovers for one or more at a time, and anything goes. We have elegant, dress-up dinner parties with the Baccarat crystal I mentioned (no, it hasn't been broken—yet), silver, china, place cards, and table decorations that Martha Stewart would envy (made by the kids). We dine to classical music and engage in intelligent conversation. At our white tablecloth dinners, we only discuss music, books, art, the theater, philosophy, or religion—but, of course, the music can be the "Rubber Ducky" song by Ernie on *Sesame Street* and the philosophy can be about gazing at the stars and trying to figure out if anyone up there is looking down at us and if anyone down here is looking up at them. Jake and I did this recently. Our conclusion: a very nice grandma on a far-away planet was sitting there with her adorable grandson wondering about life here on Earth.

But I digress. We take listening walks. We have drawing contests. We play office. One of our storage closets downstairs was transformed into an office for Jake when he requested it at the age of three. It is well stocked with play telephones, tons of paper, markers, an old credit card machine, office supplies, and a lock on the door—his idea (there had been a lot of office break-ins lately). We plant together—flowers, mostly. We have backward day and singing day. We play every kind of word game, particularly in the car. And my car is always completely outfitted for kids with extra diapers, wipes, a blanket, markers, notepads, a couple of books, Broadway show tapes, etc.

But there are other ways to be a Grandma. My sister, for instance, has five grandchildren. She's an accountant. You probably won't find a crayon in her house, she never sang or danced in her life, and she doesn't take her grandkids on endless excursions. Her grandchildren still come to her house, and they love her anyway. They find plenty to talk about, laugh about, and hug about. My girlfriend Carole lives miles and miles away from her grandchildren. But when she sees them, she makes sure to have power visits. They adore her.

So does it make me a better grandma because I invest so much in my grandchildren? God, I hope so.

Rule 26

Be prepared to prove your good driving record.

Faith lives far away from her grandchildren too (at least three of them—one newly hatched girl is close by). But back when there was only Jessica (now seven), Faith pleaded with her daughter Wendy to bring Jessica to see her, and they did when they wanted to go on a much-needed vacation. But there were *rules*. Wendy told her mother that she wasn't allowed to drive Jessie anywhere for the entire week.

"Why not?" I inquired of Faith.

"They told me I'm not a good driver," she admitted to me.

Faith, I am happy to report, has a flawless driving record and a license that is signed, sealed, and approved by the state of Pennsylvania without question. And I might add, when Faith and Mort's three daughters were young and foolish, they climbed into the back of her car time and time again without one moment's hesitation.

Well, Jessie came. Faith drove, rather than sit cooped up in her house entertaining a three-year-old for one solid week, and everyone (surprise! surprise!) survived.

Interestingly, when Jessie's mom and dad called from Rome to talk to their precious, she wouldn't come to the phone. Faith tried and tried to convince her that Mommy and Daddy were far away and missed her terribly, but no dice. Wendy and her husband flew right home that night, two days early—with that Italian leather pocketbook for Faith that I mentioned earlier.

Keep all copies of your lifetime driving record on hand for easy access. Be able to produce your license and proof of citizenship at a moment's notice. Be sure you are driving a car that *Consumer Reports* has rated the safest, or trade it in immediately. And offer up signed affidavits from neighbors and friends who will attest to your driving skills.

Rule 27

When a friend's daughter calls to ask for help, be very sure you really want to volunteer.

A visit to Grandma's can sometimes backfire. I can only tell you not to take it personally. The child is probably too young to understand that Grandma's is a haven from her annoying parents, an oasis, a port in the storm of growing up.

My friend Marcia's daughter Lynne is a new mother of five-month-old Cooper. The baby was coming to spend four days at Grandma's alone for the first time. The day before he was scheduled to arrive, Lynne called me from her home in New York to ask if I would spend at least part of Cooper's visit in Marcia's home to keep an eye on Grandma and make sure that Cooper was properly diapered, pampered, and happy. You see, I am the one with ten years' experience. I have six kidlets, and I wrote the book. Okay, I told her, not to worry. I would clear my weekend and move in with Marcia and husband Walter. "I won't take my eyes off Cooper for a second," I assured her. I know Marcia and Walter, first-time grandparents, were just dying to have me bunk in. And of course, I didn't even mention Lynne's phone call. Trust me, Marcia is quite capable. It's only her daughter who doesn't know it.

As it turned out, the joke was on me. I called Marcia on Sunday of Cooper's weekend stay and asked if she needed help. She did. In addition to five-month-old Cooper, Marcia's other grandchild, Julia Claire, was on the scene. She is two weeks younger than Cooper. By the time I got there, Marcia, a person who has never had a hair out of place and whose house is so neat it could be featured in *Better Homes and Gardens*, was exhausted and thoroughly consumed by her two grandbabies. Her husband Walter had gone off on a business trip, and she was in overdrive. She hadn't showered or eaten all day.

I found Marcia, somewhat disheveled, sitting on the floor, holding one baby who was screaming while she kept the other one in motion by rocking his jump seat with her foot.

I arrived with a bag of toys and two tapes of *Broadway*

Kids Sing Broadway, a decidedly good purchase for any grandma to have on hand.

I jumped right into the fray. I took Julia for a stroll while Marcia put Cooper in the swing, which eventually put him to sleep. We sang and danced and fed both babies. Naturally, they were hungry at the same time. I stayed four hours. Marcia kindly offered me a glass of water, which was all she could muster up, and I gladly accepted. I tried to clean up her kitchen, but she wouldn't have it.

She said, "I bet you never thought you would see my house looking such a mess." She was right.

When I got off duty, I returned home exhausted and ready for bed. However, as I told Marcia, I was happy to help because my friends were on call when I needed them early on. Now it's payback time for me.

Rule 28

If you own the offending crib, stroller, etc., be prepared never to use it for the baby. Ever.

My friend Suzie offered her kids the perfect venue for her granddaughter Arielle's first birthday party—the beach house in Brigantine, New Jersey. She hosted the in-laws, the out-laws, and a cast of thousands. Everyone, including Arielle's parents, stayed overnight. Suzie cooked herself silly, offered suitable sleeping accommodations for everyone, and made absolutely sure that not one, but both grandpas had equal time with the baby. The only problem was the guest of honor. She was having no part of Suzie's crib, lovingly bumpered and covered with coordinated clown linens.

Arielle cried herself into a frenzy the likes of which would unnerve the steeliest grandma. She emphasized her point by throwing up. She was not about to sleep in that foreign crib. Her parents (Suzie's son and daughter-in-law) deemed the culprit THE CRIB. "It was *your crib*," said Suzie to her son, in defense of the crib.

So that night, Arielle finally nodded off, safely tucked between her parents in their bed. When she was soundly asleep, her mom carefully picked her up and placed her in Suzie's crib. When this little birthday girl hit the mattress, she started wailing at the top of her lungs. And she didn't stop.

The next night, Mom and Dad begged Suzie to take Arielle into her bed so they could get a good night's sleep. Suzie, consumed with guilt over her crib, said okay.

Grandpa Ron, who has never in his fifty-nine years shared a bed with any child whomsoever, and swore he never would, protested in vain. Arielle settled in. Ron fell asleep first, Arielle second, and Suzie stayed up all night, ever conscious that if she didn't keep an eye and ear open, Arielle would get crushed or somehow crawl over 6'2" Grandpa and fall flat on the floor.

The visit ended well as long as Suzie didn't mind being sleep deprived and totally exhausted for the next seven weeks.

If you own the offending crib, stroller, high chair, car seat, or whatever, be prepared to never use it for the baby—*not once*. However, you must have these items on hand so you can impress your grandparent friends with your preparedness.

Example: I've had a booster chair on the premises since Rachel was a year old. Not one of my grandchildren has ever agreed to sit in it. They would rather sit on an ordinary chair so they can't reach the table, but can slop food all over themselves and everything within a fifty-foot radius, and sometimes fall on the floor.

I dutifully passed the booster along to my friend Marilyn when she became a grandmother. Her grandchildren don't sit in it either.

Rule 29

Birthday parties for one- and two-year-olds are irrelevant.

But the parents don't know it. My friend Carole's daughter Julie just held a birthday gala for one-year-old Derek. They had sixty guests, forty of whom were kids. Carole worked like an animal in the kitchen and Derek cried for three hours. After she came home, her Julie called her to ask if maybe all these gifts were too much, and is she teaching her son the wrong materialistic values?

Tell the mother that nobody ever died from too many toys, and the kid doesn't know what's going on anyway. It's when he is sixteen and they give him the car, the CD player, and his own TV just because it's Tuesday that the trouble begins. Don't fret. By that time, you will be dead, so it won't be your fault.

Rule 30

Don't be a dinosaur. Just be yourself.

I repeat: birthday parties for one- and two-year-olds are expensive and irrelevant and exhausting. However, the parents will have them anyway, and sometimes we grandparents play a significant part, besides washing dishes and replenishing plastic forks. This was the case with our friend Mort, Faith's husband and Jessie's grandpa.

Mort rented himself a Barney costume for $60 and showed up unannounced at Jessica's second birthday party. One look at Barney and Jessica became hysterical with fright. Mort, alias Barney, couldn't let on that it was just Grandpa trying to entertain the crowd. Jessie wanted no part of the purple dinosaur suddenly come to life, so Mort had to disappear, return the costume, and reappear as himself after the party was over. He's been in a serious funk ever since, and I'm sure when Jessie is older, she will never hear the end of it.

Rule 31

Don't make any deals you can't keep or your pocketbook can't handle.

By the time your grandchildren have civilized birthdays, their parents will tell you that the child only wants to have her friends. In other words, you're no longer invited. Good! Now you can celebrate with her alone on a special day in a special way.

When Rachel was four, she and I bought Butterscotch Krimpets (she had never tried them before) and Coke. Then we took a train ride from the nearest station to the next station, ate our snacks, got off, ran across the tracks, and hopped a train back to home base. Twenty minutes each way. She had never been on a train before, and she loved it.

Afterward we went to Zany Brainy (an educational toy store), where she picked out four presents, one for each year. Then we met Grandpa for dinner. Rachel stayed overnight—we always have birthday sleepovers—and she fell asleep holding my hand.

Every year, every birthday, my kidlets receive the number of presents to match their years. The presents don't need to be costly, and they usually are not, except for the mountain bike that Rachel requested last year. My friend Faith wondered why I didn't give her the mountain.

Rachel's friend Jennifer wanted to know if I knew when *her* birthday was—and how old she would be.

Don't make any deals you can't keep or your pocketbook can't handle. They never forget.

All our daughters and
daughters-in-law are locked
in a psychological tug-of-war.
And it's all about you.

I don't care how well they get along—and mine don't—your daughter and your daughter-in-law, or just your daughters, or all your daughters-in-law, are locked in a psychological tug-of-war. No one will ever admit it, but it's all about you. Be careful what you say to one about the other—try not to talk about much of anything other than the weather and what incredible mothers they are. And above all, do not compare their children.

No matter how you phrase it, like "Dina, your niece Rachel is in the advanced math program in school and she can pitch a softball twenty-seven miles an hour. Isn't that terrific?"

"Yes, Mom. Could you take Kelsey, *my daughter*, to ballet class on Thursday? Did I tell you her instructor says she has the best plié she's ever seen?"

Or, "Carrie, your niece Alexis is so cute. She's talking a blue streak."

"Oh? I can't understand her at all."

As for sons and sons-in-law, despite those mother-in-law jokes, this is an easier relationship all around. My son refuses to talk to me about his wife, and my son-in-law won't stop talking to me about his.

Rule 33

The only people interested in hearing about your grandchildren are grandparents who want to tell you about theirs.

Both my kids and their spouses had a third child. Matthew is now five. He told me recently that if I never, ever gave him another toy or candy or game, he would still like me—"sort of." He also mentioned that when he grows up he wants to be a movie star. Until then just give him a ball and a field and he's happy.

The third in Dina's curly-haired trio of girls is Alexis, who is now three. She is the last of the tribe. She tells everyone she is "Grandma's doll baby." I haven't said enough about Dina's middle daughter, five-year-old Amanda. She is the free spirit in the family, the artiste, and the winner of Ms. Congeniality. She gets unsolicited hugs from the other kids at preschool just because she enters the room.

And did I mention that Jake is the sweetest little boy who

ever lived, and Rachel is two grades ahead in math and wants to be a writer when she grows up, and Kelsey is so bright and beautiful she is destined to be the prom queen?

Oops, sorry! Can you imagine? I got carried away bragging about my grandchildren.

The only people interested in hearing about your grandchildren are other grandparents who want to tell you about theirs. So believe me, I'm listening hard. Suzie, Irene, Marilyn, Carole, Marcia, and Faith have all been there for me. I hope I do the same for them. Pick your audience, girls, and start your engines.

That about wraps it up for now, until I accumulate enough anecdotes for volume two. In the meantime, I'm working on *How to Be the Perfect Old Lady*, which I am rapidly becoming.

In case you were wondering why I left Grandpa out of the picture, his search for perfection takes a much different course. I think I can sum it up this way:

Rules 1 through 33 for Grandpa: Just show up!

❧ GRANDMA WHO? ☙

As this is the second edition of my book, all of us have gotten significantly older since I originally wrote the rules, and of course, my relationship with each of my six grandchildren has changed and vice versa. Rachel used to be a kid and now she is nineteen. Jake is seventeen; Kelsey, sixteen, Matt and Amanda are both fourteen; and baby Alexis is a baby no more at twelve. I am not telling you how old I am under any circumstances.

It's a funny thing, time. Just when you think you can hold the moment forever—poof! It disappears. And so do those adorable, loving grandkids who couldn't get enough sleepovers at your house, field trips to the zoo and the theater, conversations and discoveries, picnics in the bed, and elegant dress-up dinner parties in your house.

It's not that I wasn't warned. My older and wiser grandma

friends said to me, "Enjoy every single minute with your grandchildren when they are young, because along about age twelve, they will disappear." (Not all grandchildren, of course, just mine and maybe yours.)

"The window of opportunity will close," my friend Irene said. "They will want their friends, their sports, their lives, all without you."

"No way!" I shouted with confidence.

"Way!" Irene shouted back.

Well, the window not only closed. It slammed shut. Bang!

And in the case of my two grandsons, Jake (sixteen) and Matt (fourteen)—my son's sons—you could hear the big bang in China. Their older sister, nineteen-year-old Rachel, just up and went to college without even consulting me. That cute little girl who used to go on listening walks with me is now a sophomore playing rugby. I know. I know it's a brutal sport, but nobody asked my opinion.

The good news about Rachel is that we email back and forth. We have heady discussions about organic chemistry, comedy night on campus, sorority life, and those brutal rugby games. We even discuss the flu.

"A fraternity had a party last weekend and the theme was the flu," she wrote. "It was called, 'Come In Fluenza.' You had to dress as a doctor, a patient, or a nurse." College students are nothing if not creative.

At least Rachel is talking to me and she always signs off with love. Our relationship has changed, morphed to the next level. We still have silly conversations, but with a little adult tone thrown in (hers, not mine). I can no longer play Barbies with her from dawn till dusk; I am not needed to hold her in the wee hours when she's sick; I will never again ride on a train with her to the next station and back just for the fun of it.

I do not text. I cannot take pictures with my cell phone or any object other than a camera. I still talk on the phone, both landline and cell, and I am a proud emailer—there was a learning curve (mine, not hers). She is only two and a half hours away. I can visit. We are in touch. I am grateful.

We'll see where my other five grandchildren go to college. I am campaigning for my alma mater, but again, nobody asked me my opinion.

My daughter's three daughters—Kelsey (sixteen), Amanda

(fourteen), and Alexis (twelve)—do keep me in the loop. We meet for dinner once a week, and if I miss them terribly in between, I call and we chat. They rarely call me unless something monumental has occurred—like one of them got married over the weekend. Only kidding, I hope.

When Alexis made the cheerleading squad in middle school, she called to announce the big news. I did somersaults. When Amanda came home from camp, she called to say hello. I sang, "Summertime, and the Living is Easy." When Kelsey returned from a music video production workshop in New York, she rang me up.

"Guess who was in my workshop, Grandma?" she said.

"Mmm, let's see, Steven Spielberg's niece?" I said.

"Yes, how did you know?" she was shocked.

"He called yesterday."

"No he didn't," she said. "Mom must have told you."

Yes, my daughter does keep me up to date with her teenager trio, but getting any information out of my son about his sons is like pulling teeth. Our phone calls sound like this:

"Hi Michael," I say "What's new?"

"Nothing."

"How are the boys?" I ask.

"Good."

"How was Jake's trip to Australia? How was Matt's baseball camp? Basketball camp? Lacrosse camp? Football camp?"

"Good."

"Now that they're back in school, how are they doing? This is a big year for Jake, taking the SATs, looking at colleges," I say.

"Yes," he says.

"Okay," I say. "When can we get together?"

"I'll tell the boys to call you." He says.

I'm sure he does, but they don't. I call them, usually leave a message, usually never hear back.

Jake and Matt do not live six hundred miles away. It's fifteen minutes, actually. Just this week I emailed Matt the following message: "Hi Matt, I love you, I miss you. We haven't seen you or Jake for three months. So when can we get together? In the meantime I will see you next week at your football game. You might recognize me—I'll be the short, pudgy old lady with curly hair just like yours. Love ya to pieces, Grandmamma."

His answer? "ok." He didn't even use capital letters!

In those two previous conversations, phone and email, I

used 110 words. My son Michael and my grandson Matt combined used 12. Is there a serious lack of communication here or what?

But I'm the grandma. The person who for years played office with Jake when he was little, even creating a space inside a long, narrow closet in my family room for his corporate activities. We took orders for our imaginary widgets and delivered them to our imaginary customers. Our play telephones never stopped ringing. We sat on stools and shuffled papers around our pretend desks. I was basically the in-house staff, and Jake ran all over the place taking care of business. It was booming, thank you very much.

Until one day when Jake wasn't coming over as much, and our office stood empty and our customers stopped calling. We filed for bankruptcy and turned the space into storage. It was a sad day in this house.

Everyone referred to that closet as Jake's Office. And even now, filled with our boxes, suitcases, and all sorts of stuff we're saving for no good reason, we can't call it anything but "Jake's Office." I know he remembers, but we will never forget.

So one day recently I called Jake on his cell to ask about the business of his life now, and he answered.

"Hi Grandma," he said.

"Hi Jake. How are you?"

"Good."

"I miss you Jake. We haven't seen you in like, forever."

"I know. I want to show you the pictures from my trip," he said.

"Yes, I want to see and hear all about it," I said with hope in my heart. "We're free Tuesday and Wednesday this week, but if Monday, Thursday, or Friday work for you, I'll cancel my plans," I said in desperation.

"Okay, Grandma, I'll call you back," he said.

But he didn't. Now, I could chalk this up to the difference between teenage girls and teenage boys. And to make myself feel better, I did, until I heard from my friend Karen who said, "My sixteen-year-old grandson Blake had shoulder surgery today and he called me right away to tell me he was okay."

I, of course, was glad to hear it. I don't think Jake or Matt has had any operation that I should know about, but I'm certain since I last hugged them that their voices are deeper and they've grown a little taller. The rest of their lives remain a mystery to me.

As for the differences between girls and boys at this age and stage, one thing you can be sure of is that the girls will always want to go to the mall with Grandma. I have shopping trips with Kelsey, Amanda, and Alexis for their birthdays, back-to-school, starting middle school, ending middle school, starting high school, and any day that ends with the letter *y*. It's the most fun in the whole world. But my American Express card is heavily sedated at the moment. It's suffering from total exhaustion.

Don't even think about a shopping trip with the boys—they would rather chew glass.

And speaking of birthdays, the girls are a breeze to buy for: clothes, clothes, clothes.

Even Rachel, before she went back to college this year, called me and suggested a shopping trip for new clothes. This was a first for us, as Rachel is not that into clothes and shopping. So off to the mall we went. Dinner first was a pleasure. Then she picked the stores and I dragged mountains of patterned T-shirts, jeans with torn knees (you wouldn't believe the price!), and bright colored sweaters into her dressing room. She nixed it all in favor of two pairs of black jeans she needs for the campus café she works in, and three ultra plain hoodies: black, navy, and gray.

Cheapest "shopping with Grandma" date I ever had.

"That was a wonderful shopping trip, Rache," I said when we parted. At least now I know about hoodies—lighter than sweatshirts but with hoods.

"Thanks, Grandma. That was the ONLY shopping trip we've ever had," she laughed.

Teenage boys are either interested in girls or are pretending they're not. Circle your answer and return to Grandma.

Teenage girls are either definitely, positively, or absolutely interested in boys. Circle all answers.

One day I was picking up Kelsey from her after-school job and was waiting for her in front of Starbucks. Suddenly I see her walking toward me hand-in-hand with a boy, chatting away. She didn't see me at first even though I was sitting in my can't-miss-it red Volvo.

I had never seen this young man before. I didn't know he existed.

"Hi Kelsey," I said with a hug, and then I turned to the young man.

"Hi, my name is Grandma."

"Hi, my name is Austin." We shook hands and I got back in my red Volvo so they could say good-bye. I didn't look back. Honest.

Kelsey and I went off together to our favorite Japanese restaurant and we talked, talked, talked. She didn't say a word about Austin until finally I couldn't stand it any longer and I said, "Is he a secret?"

"Who?" she asked.

"Austin, that's who."

"No, he's even been to my house but my dad was throwing a fit that day about some terrible scratch on the refrigerator that nobody can see but him. That was Austin's introduction to father," she said.

"Oh, so do you want to tell me about him?" I asked.

She did.

For Grandma, it was moment when little girl Kelsey started to vanish. And I was left with the picture in my mind of the family wedding we went to when she was two, her blonde curls cascading above her beautiful bright face. She was in a perky pink dress, and the entire afternoon she ran from person to person pointing to her chubby little legs and announcing, "I got tights."

She still wears tights, but with no announcements.

Your teenage grandchildren are firmly ensconced in their worlds, and their worlds are whirling about them—"as it should be," everyone says. And they're absolutely right, but even when you've got them you don't have them.

At a holiday dinner in between bites, Alexis, who is twelve and a half, jumped up from her chair to show us a new cheer. She made the cheerleading squad in her middle school and she is consumed.

"Ready?" she asked us.

"Ready!" we chorused back.

Off she went—right, left, punching the air, kicking, turning, yelling the cheer, beaming at us, then repeating it all again.

"That's great, Alexis," I said.

She smiled, sat down, and played with her food until another cheer popped into her head and she sprang to her feet again.

Meanwhile, her fourteen-year-old sister Amanda, apropos of nothing, injected the following into the conversation: "Grandma J. [her other grandma] says Amish [long a]. How do you say it, Grandma?"

"Well, I always say, *Ahhh-mish*," I replied, wondering what this had to do with anything.

It doesn't. It only proves that teenagers are on a different wave length than the rest of us, so just deal with it. There was no more attention given the Amish situation, so everyone went back to eating and discussing more pertinent subjects, like "Why doesn't Alexis stop cheering every five minutes?" Amanda said of her sister. "I'm so bored with it."

My friend Irene, the older and wiser one, has four grand-children scattered all over the country, all with self-supporting careers except for the youngest, Shane, who is in law school. Shane still calls and talks to Irene on occasion.

"She still needs me," Irene said. "I'm the only thing standing between her and her mother" (Irene's daughter). "Conflict resolution is my specialty."

We grandmas do have our specialties, but what used to be isn't anymore. Try to stay in the moment. Stay in contact with your grandchildren no matter how many phone calls go unanswered. Use any form of communication you can find: snail mail, email, telephone, telegraph, carrier pigeon, shouting from your rooftop. If all else fails, send them a check for $100. Sometimes that gets their attention.

If you live nearby and they play sports, go to their games as often as possible. They won't see you in the stands, but you'll see them on the field. Then after the game chase after them like a grandma groupie.

"Good game, Matt," I said as I patted him on his shoulder pad.

"Uh, thanks Grandma," and he disappeared with his teammates into the locker room.

You can vary it with "Great game, Matt," but you'll get the same response.

Grandmas of the world: Unite! Stay strong. Don't panic. Keep busy with your own life. And if you are very, very lucky, someday your adorable, loving grandchildren will come back. All it takes is time.

I'm waiting.

ABOUT THE AUTHOR

Bryna Nelson Paston is an overjoyed grandmother of six, aged twenty to twenty-seven, whom she calls the music of her universe. Formerly an editor of a local weekly newspaper in Philadelphia, she has written for numerous national magazines and newspapers. Bryna has also written and published multiple children's plays. She lives in Elkins Park, Pennsylvania.